The

Dictator

and the

Heretic

A Collection of Poems
by Momodou Sallah

Global Hands Publishing 2018

The Dictator and the Heritic is published by:

Global Hands Publishing
Voluntary Action Leicester
9 Newarke Street, LE1 4SN
Tel: 01162577952
Email: publishing@global-hands.co.uk
Web: www.global-hands.co.uk

Typeset by:	Global Hands Publishing
Cover Design by:	Jaana Ojakäär-Kitsing
Cover illustration by:	Brandboard Creative

Copyright © 2018 Momodou Sallah

A catalogue record for this book is available from the British Library

ISBN: 978-0-9956460-2-5

Dedicated to

All Global Hand members, volunteers, supporters; past and present.

About the Author

Momodou Sallah (PhD) teaches at the Social Work, Youth and Community Division, De Montfort University, UK. He is a founding director of Global Hands, a Social Enterprise/Charity operating in The Gambia and UK, with a focus on capacity building and social good. He has more than 20 years' experience working with young people at local, national and international levels; from being the Youth Director of Gambia Red Cross Society to a Senior Youth Worker at the Leicester City Council, UK. In November 2015, he was named the "Most Innovative Teacher" in the UK by Times Higher. His passion is poetry, and this is his second collection of poems, following the release of his first poetry book *Innocent Questions,* in 2012. Momodou has also written or edited four other academic books. He has developed an avid interest in farming and now considers himself a farmer.

Table of Contents

Preface

This collection of 19 poems promotes heresy against what Paula Freire (1972) calls the "defective logic of the system", unashamedly. I have been struck in my praxis by how individuals and communities I have worked with are afflicted by the poverty of the imagination, by a corrosive lack of belief in their abilities, to transform their lives, manifested both in gradual and residual exactitudes.

Boaventura de Sousa Santos (2014) recognises a causal nexus as "cognitive injustice" which affects a significant proportion of those living in the South; this incapacitates people as the dominant ways of knowing and being, do not find these Southern perspectives 'credible or visible'; he calls for epistemologies of the South, to counter this. The question then becomes: how do we disrupt dominant ways of knowing and being? One way for me, through this book, is the art of exposition and provocation of critical consciousness.

To question the dictator, perhaps society and normality, is to invite terrible visitations on the self and the community; it can be a dark, desolate and lonely island, without much company. Heretics can be construed as mad, deviant and troublesome when in fact, it is society that is walking on its head and waving its arms as legs, deluded that it is normal and that all contradictory views are abnormal, for that is the way of the dictator.

To confront the beastly dictator is to invite pain that cannot even be imaged; the beast will come back at you in all its ugliness, if you wag its tail. It demands "objectivity" and "neutrality" that treats every challenge as an existential threat. Therefore, to confront the beast of dictatorship requires reflexibility, tact, flexibility, discipline, determination, democracy, strategy and the willingness to pay the ultimate price of freedom, death.

I must confess that I write for myself first and foremost, to make sense of the world, to decipher the dysfunctional normality that beguiles me, and to prostrate heretic attempts at engendering pedagogies of disruption. As a poet, I am imbued with the struggles in my environment; the blood, sweat and tears of my home becomes the tapestry of my art, I cannot be divorced from this construction of reality and the suffering of my people. Consequently, my art is both a protest against the dictator as well as therapeutic intervention for my sanity; both positioned as acts of resistance.

I hope this collection of poems inspires heretics and young aspiring revolutionaries to conceptualise heresy against the logic of the system as reasonable; in fact, it is a prerequisite for proposing a more just and equitable counter narrative. I also hope that it motivates them to learn the new martial arts; and as has been said, to be water!

Momodou Sallah
September 2018, Leicester, UK

Reference
Freire, P. (1972) Pedagogy of the Oppressed, Harmondsworth, Penguin.

De Sousa Santos, B. (2014) Epistemologies of the South. Justice against Epistemicide.
Boulder/London: Paradigm Publishers.

Children of the naked emperor

Ants lead lions into battle
Fig leaves, olive branches
Truth is a feast and famine
Only licking appeases the beast
Grovelling
Plebs rain confetti
On the emperor's footsteps
Burkina Faso is a wasteland
The children heaved
In sync with the
Whine and whim
Of the emperor's delusion grandeur.

The swiftness of the samurai guillotine
Minions in his dominion
Roast the timeline
The bees attacked
The perfume drenched emperor
Only the stench
Of his rotten flesh
Repels them.

The children crawl on his word
And drink his piss
Licking lips, vigorously
Eating his shit in glee
Rushing to catch his vomit
With palms stretched to the heavens.

In the great land of the mighty emperor
He feeds on the fear of the children
In pointing, he pierces the sky
His shroud, *ninkinanka*
Tiki taka
Tip tap, his mysticism
Creeps
Pictures paint the sky
Dye, die
Hi, bye
We lie
Under
Mile 2 sky.

Bambadinka
Imams raped
Crocodiles feasted
10 men plunged into innocence
Violently
Vigorously
Wailing veil
In Mozart's midnight scream
Crescendo dream.

White elephants
Ceremonial regalia
One-minute dung
Public toilet
Damaged goods
Jeefee Jaafaa
Crowned clown
Paper tiger
Hype rider.

Press gagged
Soap barred
Opposition tarred
Head shattered
Hope Staggered
Hubris starred.

Heretics will be roasted
Idiots will be boosted
Cobwebs hide the dusty roads
Breathing in *kubay jara*
Mediocrity three times a day
Hand to mouth, day to day
Praise be to the Most High.

The sun, the nun

The high, the low
And the so-so
The rough, the tough
And no dough
The bad, the ugly
So ho ho
The grief, the brief
Wai yai yo
The hump, the dump
All go-go
The slick, the lick
It's promo
The prick, the sick
No more oh
The struggle, the bubble
Go home now
The new, the hew
All same oh
The race, the base
No grace woo
The haze, the maze
All lost so
The game, the tame
All hush hush
The task, the tusk
Same pierce oh
The sun, the nun
Still pure woo.

Feast of the maggots

Flies feast
On the rotten flesh
Before we lick
The bottom of the bowl
Wounded roads
Bite buttocks
Toads roar in the harmattan
Pot bellies burst like blisters
The stench of the decayed living
Fertilizes the bloated soil
Ruptured boil
The lungs of the grave
Drink the puss of the wretched
Vomiting green maggots
And *dunkolong*.

From the crossing
To the back way
Stealing is good
Corruption nourishes
The wall grows, virtue dies
The aircon cuts off
The flow of blood, to the brain
Clotted arteries
Oozing and gushing
To irrigate.

Banal decadence
Virtual lenses, twisted view
Jum is a prisoner
Mansa bengo of rats, cockroaches and vultures
Power tricks and polyandry.
We have no shame
We have no game.

The necktie chokes
Slavery vogues
Still broods
Reality is borrowed
Introverted
Hell triggered
The results are rigged
They can only go
One way
Another way.

Death eats the patients
Sellers have been sold
Jalangs have never foretold
The peanuts grow cancer
Tribe is banter no more
The market is constipated
Hewers of wood
Drink your piss
Let the vultures
Desecrate your carcass
Feast of the maggots.

Goodbye my friend

Treachery flashes
Convoluted realities unfold
Images of dark currents
The sea and the sand
The sun shines, illuminates
I stand under the heavenly radiance of the sun
My sins washed and my heart pure
Anger is a foreigner
Disappointment is an illegal alien
I bow unconditionally
I exit without emotion
Goodbye my friend.

Though my heart is heavy
And rivers flow from my eyes
Though melancholic fumes choke me
Though dreams and nightmares constellate
The clarity of the Northern star
Consumes me
A void now exists
Transcending existentialism
Descending into a place
That is nowhere
Somewhere
Beyond the present
Beyond the future
Beyond yesteryears
Somewhere
Words cannot capture
Zen.

Even though I gave you
My heart and soul
Without condition
Even though
I will still swallow
A thousand embers for you
Even though I will walk
A thousand thorny Milky Ways
And back
I will not wallow in this quagmire
Anymore
I must love you more than myself
And pay love's butcher's bill
I must leave you
In a leap of faith
Goodbye my friend.

The Goats ran away

Anger twinges at the heart of my soul
Rubbing, scratching, screeching and breaching
The man insists on selling me melanin
Unleashes his cancer worms
To sell me mirages
Of melons
Under the midday sun
She kisses me with backstabs
And tells me
That the pain is only imaginary
He weaves his web of lies
Around my soul
And soothes me
With mediocrity
That insults me.

The goats ran away
My sweat is swayed
The money ran away
I gave it to the head,
The head gave it to the tail
And the tail ate it
It disappeared
Into thin air
The prices double
And the labour dwindled
My prize is a double pregnancy.

They quench their thirst
With the sweat of the nation
Wenching on the nation's souls
They chew the thighs
Of the baby
Issssssss
And suck his marrow
With a juicy smile
On their bloodied lips
Their tears lubricate the rape
The living dead roam the streets
A drought of tears
Deny them release.
You rock to the beat
Of the wailing children
Whilst I toil
To feed your soil.

You eat the aid of the people
AIDs has nothing on you
You hide behind the sanctity of truth
To dement and torment
The hopes of people
You tell me stories
Of money growing legs
And walking away
In broad daylight.

Enough of these stories
Of escaped goats
And hanging donkeys
I could not find
A particle of remorse
In your space
A spectre of dignity
In your hands
This sceptre you hold
Has no shame
I am now allergic
To your excuses
Your obesity is based
On the Kwashiorkor of our people.

The zombies used to eat
In the secrecy of the night
Now they chew the babies
In broad daylight
Without remorse
The dark arts are pervasive
Celebrated and worshipped
They feed off my soul
Dementors sucking
On my family's happiness
I search in vain
For the antidote
To shackle
The cannibals
In vain.

The people race
Against funeral of month
To evade death
This twisted normality
Beguiles me
I toil and soil
To reach the mountain town
Whilst ten consecrate
Ten desecrate
Simultaneously
The breath is frozen
The status quo
Remains stagnant
Phantom of the talkers
And of few doers.

Pagan temple

As I stand in the annals of civilisation
The beginning before creation
Existential questions bite my soul
Tributaries flow
To different paradigms
As I search the mountain tops
The heavens hold mystery
The craters moulded history
The future shrouded
In a leap of faith.

Deciphering hieroglyphs
Obstacle of boulders
Of biblical Argentinosaurus
Am I?
I am?
What am I?
How has it come to be?
They asked for the images
Fingers on lips tasked sages
Dictum desecrated
By the holy savages
I am at one
The force is around me
Within me.

In the trance of suffering
I seek transcendence
The food of the mind fuels me
Eschew metaphysical forces
Chew natural herbs
I am in a higher place
A higher plane
I levitate without gravity
In a deep space
Beyond the eyes
Absorbing and morphing
In this cosmic energy
Beyond space, beyond time.

The bird eats the worms
The man eats the birds
The worms eat the man
I don't need to be
I am.

The dictator and the heretic

The heretic spoke
His mind
And treaded
On the abnormal
Normality
The other one
Huffed and puffed
And threw him
All the way out.

Silence
Heavy silence
Hangs in the air
All eyes looked
Away
We have not seen
The sparkling blade
In the middle of the night
There!
The sun is not there!

Conscience wrestles
With economics
Dignity fits
With servitude
Baa baa Black sheep
We have no wood
And we have no food
Chaff is gold
Silence is golden.

As aliens compete
For the cruelty trophy
To show the God
Who is the cruellest
Of them all
Servants manoeuvre
To navigate
The daily perils
Of the dictatorship.

You know that you do not know

You know that you do not know
When our sweats are dews
Dripping on the floor of the Sahara heat
When we wake up
From our nightmares
With hoarse voices
When bloodstains remain
In the fleeting interval
Of our induced state
Of false consciousness
And we see the internal bleeding
Of our intestines, of our brains
When the national conscience
Haemorrhages
When hegemony is a new normality
When it is easier to know
That you do not know
When the mind is imprisoned
And spatiality and geography
Cannot unbolt the prison doors
Of our mind.

You know that you do not know
As they fight for our hearts and minds
They take our bodies and souls too
In a country where we are whores of tyranny
And climax to the daily doses of violence
That is injected into our nervous system
Where heretics and lunatics
Rule the world
Where criticality and consciousness

Are devoid of your existence
Where ignorance
Is the anchor
That weighs us down
You know that you do not know.

You know that you do not know
As cyber warriors masturbate
On their keyboards
From afar
And lose themselves
In the ferocity
Of the five-knuckle shuffle
From distant lands
And spew infertility
In liquid modernity
Barren food on the ground
The heroes and sheroes
Strive for daily survival
And navigate
Dangerous rapids
And some fall off
And some quit just being
A country burns.

As the constitution is desecrated
And parliament is a gathering
Of cockroaches and vultures
As the press is ripped apart
Block by block
As a country suffers in silence

Bitten many times
By the economic shark
As a man imposes himself
On the psyche of a nation
Bludgeoning, impaling, shafting,
As the people navigate
The treacherous waters
Of the politics
Of bread and butter
As no one stands up, everyone falls
You know that you do not know.

You know that you do not know
Where to be
Is not to speak
And where to speak
Is not to be
Where what was not
To be
Is now being
Can now be
Has now to be
Must be.

You know that you do not know
Fear eats my courage
On a daily basis
And I cannot stand and fight
Shadows who shout
From afar
And impotent bulldogs
Death is my companion

Death starks me
In the deepest valleys and crevices
Tears do not wipe away
The shame
Hopelessness is what gives me
A high
It is my comfort zone.

I know that you do not know
To stop to point a finger
Is to invite things
That you do not know
And things you do not know
You can only imagine
And things you can only imagine
Exist only in Alcatraz.

I know that you do not know
Fear paralyses
Fear of the unknown
Incapacitates
I eat fear
I drink fear
I sleep with fear
I am fear.

I know that you do not know
This disease seeps deep
Into our psyche
And saps our dignity
Because oblivion is bliss
When to know

Is to court death
Because hiding from myself
Is an easier path
And the heart beat
Must be mortgaged
Against silence
Confrontation is suicide,
Compromise ....
Is another payday loan
With a 2000% APR
When once mighty ones
Have fallen
And we lesser ones
Who stand on their backs
Can only falter
When prophets and judges
Sell their souls.

I know that you do not know
The tectonic plates
That once held this country
Together
Are being ripped apart
In broad daylight
The intellectuals hide
Behind their books and glasses
The wigs, gavel, gowns and clowns.
I cannot separate
Behind a tainted law
A dirtied law
As the clergy sit

On their folded holy books
Stuffed notes
Obliterating their silence
Their covenant with the Almighty
Now a convenience
Only a few of conscience
Struggle to sleep
Engulfed in a state
Of catatonic catastasis
As the siren pierces the air
And the conductor orchestrates
The symphony
Of the possessed
In deep slumber land.

Death is the price of freedom

The nostrils of the earth
Corruption stained
Death is the price of freedom
The ancestors demand
Blood be spilt
To fertilize
The womb of this change.

Open air prisons
Mouths gagged with barbwire
Fear liberated, terrorised
A heartless system
Without heartbeat
Without conscience, sucks
And without consent, fucks.

My pleasure is your pain
My sane is your bane
My high is your hype
My boo is your zoo
My loot is your shoot
My wine is your whine
My cane is your chain
Why would I give it up?

Freedom
Is the final frontier
In this realm
Or another dimension
The leg
That cannot straighten
Must be broken
Against the world
We have no other place
To go
But forward.

The shackles in my head
Disruption
Transcendence
The duality of existence
Fight or flight
Exorcise yourself
With your own blood
Death is the price of freedom.

lisboa

The old bricks built
From the plunder
Of the ancient empire
Crumbles
Tumbling
From the massive dosage
Of capitalism
One million people
Throng the streets of Lisboa
Palpable anger hit me in the face.

The *Aluta continua* strikes
The core of my heart
Breaks into the rhythm of my heart
Beats with the rhythm of Ireland
Beats with the rhythm of Greece
Beats with the rhythm of Italy
Beats with the rhythm of Fado
Breaks into the rhythm
Of the 75% failure rate
The golden shackles
Suffocate the sick
In their homes.

I stand in the ocean
I stand on the ocean
I feel the breeze of the Atlantic
An ancient port of plunder
The ruinous buildings
Trap the heat
That smothers the people
Marching and marching
Up economic outrage.

The rhythm of
The downtrodden
Reverberates
Through the streets of Lisbon
The stench of the corpses
Rise up
From the ancient empire
The foundation built
On the plundered corpses
Cackle and buckle.

Only the height of vantage
Reveals the depth of despair
The birds scatter into the sky
And the feet and hands
Left anchored in the abyss
In the floods
But this heartbeat
Is a universal heartbeat
That transcends
The flags of nations.

I must run away

Let frustration creep
Let it creep, let it creep
Let it rise
Let the hearts be empty
Let us empty our hearts
Let our nostrils flare
Let us tear out our intestines
We will not live again
Let us rip our hearts from our chest
And throw it or chew it.

Let frustration creep
Let it creep, let it creep
Every day, every night,
Every second, every minute
Let frustration creep for eternity
Let blighted, blocked horizons rise
Let the blighted horizons be unblocked
Let it creep
Let frustration stay how it is
Let it stay how it is
Let us rise, let us stay, let us die
Let us live.

Born, live and die
In this frustrated hell
This concrete jungle
Where roses shall not grow
Where fruits shall not germinate.
Let me scratch my head bloody
Let my nails dig into my head
Let my heart burst open
Let the monotony consume me, consume me
Without anywhere to look
Let the monotony consume me
May the repetition
Last forever
And ever.

The souls that rise will be gunned
The flowers that blossom will be clipped
The petals shall be infested
And they shall live in hopelessness
Let the grey sky cook me monotony
As I soliloquise
Let melancholy fuck me all over
Let the hopes be drained
And the future be sprained
Give me death, let me eat death
Death would be a better place
Bushmen, cavemen, live a better life
To hope is to transgress,
To believe is to be a heretic
They shoot me down with a 1000 guns,
But I wanna rise but I cannot rise
Because they shoot me down with a 1000 guns

I am a mad man, I am a mad man
This normality I do not understand
This normality woos me
This normality ...
What is this normality again?
I breathe the rhythm of the streets, fumes
I go nowhere, I stand nowhere, I am nobody
I cannot be
I am undefined
I am indefinable
I am unharnessed
I am uncultivatable
I have no milk and honey
The flowing land is only a distant mirage
We witness heaven and hell
Right here, right now
Everyday.

Pourquoi mon ami,
Pourquoi parles-tu toujours des blessés et de la mort?
Pour qui?
My friend you do not understand
Because my vocabulary
Is defined by who I am
What I eat
My vocabulary is who I am
Because of what I wear
Everyday
In my vocabulary, there are no flowers
In my vocabulary, there is only blood
Painted blood

Blood that paints the streets
And the tattooed trees
Blood that paints the lives, the hopes
The dreams, the shit,
So this is the painted blood
So my vocabulary must be about blood
And pain, and suffering, and tears, red tears
My art is defined by my environment
I draw from the dark arts
To draw eternal damnation
Let this uncultured soliloquy
Hit you in the head
May you rest never, forever.

I cannot live like this
I call on you death to come and take me
Take me away, far away
Where my eyes will be closed forever
Forever and ever
They tell me that it is the throne or the grave
But I don't want the grave
But I don't want the throne
I want to live
Because I am a dead man walking
Walking corpse interacting
People think I am alive
But I am dead, my blood is not flowing
My heart is not beating
I am standing here with nothing to do
Let me shake but you will not feel the pain
You do not feel the rhythm
The incessant scream of the kids.

Wants to drive me mad
I want to run away
I want to run away from this place
Let me rise
There is no food in this house
And even the garbage is empty
The pain is a long, unwinding
Never ending path that must be travelled
On a daily basis
And repeated at the end of exhaustion
Maya tells I rise
But even she could not rise from this weight
They tell me that no matter
How wide the mouth of the river is
It is scalable
But this is not scalable
On a rector scale, it is blown off
We do not have the instruments
And the vocabulary
To measure pain on this scale.

My pain and my rage
Conflate to eat me
That there is another place
That I do not know
What it looks like, what it feels like
What it would be
What I know is that I live now
Pain, train, faint, taint, rain, pain
What I know is that ....
Let me escape from this place

Let me go to another world
Let me go somewhere
Just anywhere.

Let us dig deep into the psyche
The metaphysical must somehow
Be present
The combobulation must somehow burst
Like a blister
I must deliver and be delivered
Somehow this pregnancy must end
Somehow the blister must burst
Somehow we have to escape
And let me tell you
Getting high, and licking, and sniffing
And ticking and injecting
Are all temporary measures
And they cannot take away my pain
Because they can only serve
On a temporary basis
And elevate me to the most high place
The itching is the bank of a 1000 lies
I must run away from this place
I must eat the bites of the vampire
She eats my flesh whilst I still stand
She turns my head around
And pretends to blow
Whilst she is still biting me
The mice bites and blows, bites and blows
Bites and blows
The hostages stand harmless

And innocent
The whining of the mosquitoes
The whining of the mosquitoes
The whining of the mosquitoes
They drive me mad
I am in a nuthouse
They never shut up
They go on and on and on and on
I want to end it
I don't want to hear all these voices in my head
Again, again, again, again
I just wanna go somewhere and end it
My untamed attack dogs, the hounds of hell
They bite me on a daily basis
From far away
Maya, I told you there is no rising again
You cannot rise from this
You just have to lie and die
The never-ending queue, they take their bite
One after the other
And every day, I sit down there
And they suck every bit of their pound of flesh
And once they are done
Sucking their pound of flesh
I have to regenerate every day
Again and again
To get it again in the morning
I cannot give anymore pounds of flesh
But there is no end
To this long horizon's queue
The machines, the chemicals and the cancer
I must run away.

Basket on the head

Basket on the head
Hope in the clouds
Akimbo in limbo
Kwashiorkor in bimbo
Heaps of debasement
Saltless paltry
Selfish deities
Dignified island.

Raba raba
Taf taf
Thieves guffaw
Freedoms emasculated
Elasticated lies
Disappearing pies
Lice and mice
Zum zum
Zam zam.

Mighty sweats
Meagre sweets
Puppet puppies
Zombie masters
Drinking fumes
Shitting blood.

Traffic din
Pocket *jinns*
Bucket list
Filthy paws bite
The earth's bosom
Neverdie blossoms.

She plays the strings of my heart

She plays the strings of my heart
We make musical sounds
And ride the waves
She teaches me to giggle
In our bubble
Hobbling in our heresy
Deaf to the eyes of the world.

No licking she told me
Just tickling
The load on our shoulders is diddle
Let's be single and mingle
Judgment day is a hoax
Forget your Botox.

Inhale the grass
Exhale the brass
Eat Banksy
Be sexy
She sings
These soothing songs
In my soul.

Your thorns prick my heart

Your thorns prick my heart
Drip, drip,
The pain flows
There is no glow
In the darkness
Tip tap, tip tap
In the emptiness.

Boom, boom
Boomerang
Diss, piss
And puss
Mist and hiss ....
The least
Of the beast.

Toss
And start
Only the competitor
Can taste defeat
Slow the heartbeat
Let the bullets fly.

Hate

Hate, hate
Come again
Never again
Brain, chain, rain
All night pain, stain
Heart, hate
Hiss, hurt, hurl
Invectives, injection, Invictus
Sand, storm, bomb.

The heart is painted
With the blood of the roses
The eyes can
Only see
The red mist
There is only sin
In the dictionary
Prison
It is a constant state of war, whore!

Levitate

Beyond the realms of mortality
A new code of morality
A saint is born
A sinner is done.

Zen in the war zone
Zombie flesh zero
Cosmic clarity
Corpse with makeup.

Dark self, true self
A thousand miles
Is one metre
Producers and consumers.

Tillers and eaters
Emotions are programmed
Feelings commodified
Levitate, gravitate.

I am
Because I am not
Fast food junky
System donkey
Jester's monkey

Dancing bear
Drink beer
Hollowed laughter
Fake news, fake smile
Know thyself
Smoke the truth
Dignity and distribution.

Wele wele

Machine gun mouth, mosquito legs
Shit lover, smell dodger
Big mouth, small hands
Stinky lyrics, sticky rhymes
Smelly matrix, pillow overload.

Wele, wele, *gele gele*
Ruble rouser, hope douser
Okra mouth, barbwire bout
Makeup artist, breakup mortician
Umul bebarr, talking drum.

Step on cockroaches, tire necklacing
Market brawl, troll crawls
War starts, Satan absconds
Bullet fired, mullet smashed
Machete chops, bloodletting.

Midnight bukarabu

Chakras open
Shackles off
Losing myself
In the beat
Of the midnight bukarabu
Rhythmic vibration
Tantric pulsation
Third eye entrance.

Achum
Mystical rhythm
Devine symmetry
Rhyme and rhythm
Trance, dance
Beads, *keseng keseng*
Floating on bars
Agent provocateur
Silent killer
Intoxicant, no toxins.

Creator's creation
Structural integrity
Constructive alignment
Sculpture's paradise
Oneness
Atoms yearn for
Cosmic unification
Devine intervention.

Tribal dance

Subtle, supple
Like water
Devastating, dehumanizing
Like tsunami
Hidden, invisible
Like the mist
Palpable, attention seeking
Like a cyclone
Ungovernable, unpredictable
Like British weather
Regimented, structured
Like a platoon of lagoons.

Change form, change rhythm
Pour the bleach
Wailing dance, mournful gyrate
Drowned drumming
Shifting goalposts, mutating beat
Stunted daze
Calibrated celebration, tribal warriors
Wriggle and rig
Stick and drum, drum and drummer
Slave and master.

Game untamed, shame unnamed
Hate heralded, dignity desecrated
Wrist slashed, waist gyrates
Midnight tears, daylight robbery
Drinking bleach in bliss
Dancing to the beat of the tribal privilege.

Glossary of terms (in alphabetical order)

Achum - *An exclamation, often of joy, showing appreciation for something.*

Aluta continua - *Portuguese word referring to the struggle continues, steeped in Mozambique's war of liberation*

Bambadinka - *Situated in the Old Jeshwang prison in The Gambia; it was said to be The Gambia's hell on earth.*

Bukarabu - *A set of drums, three or more that is played, with the drummer sometimes wearing beads around the wrists. It is commonly known to be played by the Jola tribe in the Senegambia area.*

Dunkolong – *The sound of big, massive faeces dropping in the toilet.*

Gele gele - *Public transport minibus that can carry 18-22 passengers and is often in a poor state of repair.*

Jalang - *A deity in traditional religion which is worshipped.*

Jeefee Jaafaa - *The sound and act of making something disappear, in the blink of an eye. Acts of magic and possible hoodwink.*

Jinns - *Mystical creatures, that can be good or bad, who can make themselves visible to humans.*

Jum - *There is no exact translation of the Wollof word in English, but it combines attributes of honesty, virtue, integrity, loyalty and reciprocity.*

Keseng keseng - *Onomatopoeia, sound of beads either around the wrist or the waist, jiggling.*

Kubay jara - *Literal translation in Mandinka is "fixer of all things"; a plant that is a hallucinogen.*

Mansa bengo - Gathering of the kings.

Neverdie - It is a plant that has the ability to survive under extreme conditions and has great healing properties. The scienctific name is Moringa oleifera

Ninkinanka - A mystical beast in The Gambia akin to a dragon that is rarely seen but lives both in water and land.

Tiki taka - Wollof word meaning to untie and then to tie again, it is also an onomatopoeia.

Umul hebarr - Radio kang kang, distributor of false news.

Wai yai yo - A cry for help invoking the name of mum.

Wele wele - the sound of talking, mostly empty words.

Zam zam - The zam zam well is located in Masjid al-Haram in Mecca, Saudi Arabia; 20 metres from the holy Kaaba, the holiest place in Islam. The water is considered holy and millions of people go there every year to drink from it.

Zum zum - Highly potent locally made gin in the Gambia whose intoxicating powers are immediate and extremely high. It is highly addictive and is highly frowned upon especially for Muslims to drink.

OTHER BOOKS BY GLOBAL HANDS PUBLISHING

A Geocritical Representation of Banjul (Bathurst): 1816-2016

Pierre Gomez and Hassoum Ceesay (Editors)

The book is a refreshing, if not seminal, addition to Gambian Studies in that it is the first tome to specifically address aspects on the history and society of Banjul, The Gambian capital since its purchase by the British in 1816. The various authors have taken a multidisciplinary approach to unravel the salient role of The Gambian capital in the making of the colonial heritage of the country. Indeed, although the chapters specifically address issues related to Banjul, the larger history of the country unravels as one goes through the monograph. This book explores the Gambian capital with a view to making a logical and rational explanation of its dynamics.

Rarely has a West African city gotten a whole book dedicated to her history, and this book is therefore a real masterstroke in innovative scholarship which all students of Gambian history should read.

Profiles of Gambian Political Leaders in the Decolonisation Era (2017)

Jeggan Senghor (Editor)

Profiles of Gambian Political Leaders in the Decolonisation Era provides an insightful and educational account into the achievements, flaws and lives of four key Gambian leaders; the book is an exploration of how their influence transcends their own lifetimes and informs crucial aspects of The Gambia today.

Spanning a history of over one hundred years, from the 1870s to the 1990s, the biographies follow the decolonisation process and presents portraits of four political leaders, namely, Samuel J. Forster, Edward F. Small, John C. Faye, and Pierre S. Njie, together with commentaries in the preface, the introduction, and the postscript. For each, involvement in the politics of the day is fundamental and, therefore, extensively discussed, particularly the contributions to the creation and management of political parties and organisations, formal and non-formal relationships between parties and, most important, relationships with the colonial order and its agents.

In each of the four cases the narrative goes beyond the purely political and examines in some detail the personal, social, and roles played in other walks of life in which the individual was involved. The end result is a more total picture of the man seen through his inputs to the process of defining and implementing the national political agenda.

This edited collection would be suitable for any reader or scholar familiar with the works of these writers, interested in these fascinating political individuals or in African colonial and postcolonial studies.

Before the New Earth: African Short Stories

Tijan M. Sallah

In this book, Tijan M. Sallah has written a remarkable first collection of African short stories. It is a landmark of Gambian literature. Steeped firmly in the tiny country's experience, the narratives present the moral tales of a society dealing with life and death, family life, social injustice, crime and punishment, and the moral dilemmas of living in a contemporary African society. The characters engage in complex human relationships and want a better world, a new earth.

Gendered Voices From The Gambia (2015)

Pierre Gomez and Isatou Ndow (Editors)

This book builds on the growing academic literature on gender. It draws on a number of Gambian works to analyse gender in contemporary Gambian fiction. It focuses on challenging the social construction of gender norms, inequality and abuse whilst analysing how gender norms and stereotypes are represented, reinforced and challenged in significant facets of Gambian literature. A useful book for students, scholars and lay persons interested in African literature, gender studies and Gambian studies.

Patriots: Profiles of Eminent Gambians (2015)

Hassoum Ceesay

This book captures the history of The Gambia over the past three hundred years through the life stories of men and women who have helped to shape the destiny of the country. A journey through this volume leads to a critical understanding of Gambian history, spanning the pre-colonial slave trade to resistance to European penetration, to the era of colonial rule; to the nationalist awakening leading to independence.

Baaba Sillah: Reclaiming the Mantle (2015)

Pierre Gomez and Malang Fanneh (Editors)

Time travelling through the annals of history, Baaba Sillah stands tall as a literary giant for whom the communication of historical insights constitute both a passion and preoccupation. In this book, Gomez and Fanneh have used a holistic thematic approach to examine a myriad of historical, political, socio-economic and cultural themes that are explored in the works of Sillah. It explores the dynamics of gender, culture and power relations in both the colonial and post-colonial Gambian society.

Harrow: London Poems of Convalescence (2014)
Tijan M. Sallah

Harrow: London Poems of Convalescence is a unique collection of poems from the renowned Gambian writer. Rhyming, simple and reflective, they depart from the poet's usual free verse. The poems deal with the near-death experience of a pedestrian hit by a car in London, the agony of pain in recovery and finally, the magic of healing. It is poetry geared towards a private function, quite unlike his other poems, which extol either Gambian Wolof values or criticize American racism and materialism.

Harvest of Gambian Lines: An Anthology of Poems (2014)
Abdoulie Jatta and Musa Jallow (Editors)

These poems offer a vision of the world beyond the physical sense, where the seed of peace germinates and breaks into leaf to line the walls of faith and selfhood. This is an anthology that demonstrates what happens when writing is dedicated to socio-political and economical changes; particularly concerning the issues that many Africans face: debt; religiosity; poverty; venality of rulers and the betrayal and threat to innocence. These poets bear witness to the interior landscape of the cellular workshop of their very beings.

The Graveyard Cannot Pray (2013)

Baba Galleh Jallow

This book is an autobiographical account of one man's battle to save his daughter from female circumcision. A struggle that is defiant of a harmful traditional practice and defective constructions of normality. This is perhaps the first autobiographical account of a male perspective articulating to battle against Female Genital Mutilation. The Graveyard Cannot Pray throws into sharp relief four interconnected phenomena: the conflict between an older and younger generation; the communal nature of conflict and resolution among the Futa Fulani; the Fulani notion of son-hood, and the potential complications that arise when the sanctity of tradition is stood in opposition against the sanctity of faith.

Innocent Questions (2012)

Momodou Sallah

This collection of poems harnesses the theme of struggle in a way very few writers have been able to. The author combines his background of growing up in The Gambia and an adult life residing in the UK to great effect: a fusion of writing styles and constructed realities. The poems in this collection jump from the pages and evoke palpable emotions. This collection of thirty-two poems explores a range of pertinent issues with a complex simplicity that is dramatic and mesmerising; from the dreams of an African schoolboy to the frustrations of a consummate professional in Babylon.